Planet of the Zombie Zonnets

Seasons One and Two

Juan Manuel Pérez

Planet of the Zombie Zonnets

Seasons One and Two

Juan Manuel Pérez

A Zombie Texas Poet of The Year

Copyright © 2021 Juan Manuel Pérez

All rights reserved. No part of this book may be reproduced, stored in a retreival system, or transmitted by any means, electronic, mechanical, photocopying, recording, or otherwise, without written permission from the author.

ISBN: 978-1-7350976-2-6
(Hungry Buzzard Press)

Published by:

Hungry Buzzard Press
P.O. Box 80164
Keller, TX 76248-2300

The poems entombed within have appeared in the following magazines, webzines, blogs, and anthologies:

At Home Anthology
Boundless: The Anthology Of The Rio Grande Valley International Poetry Festival
Bleached Butterfly
Blood Moon Rising Magazine
Corpus Christi Writers Anthology
Fallen Angel Poetry Facebook Group Page
Harbinger Asylum
Horror Writers Association Online
Red Planet Magazine
Poetry Society Of Texas Facebook Group Page
Poetry Superhighway Facebook Group Page
Poetry Universe Facebook Group Page
Rat's Ass Review
Rattle's Anything Goes Poetry Facebook Group Page
Red River Review
Screw The Wall! And Other Brown People Poems
Speculations II: Poetry From The Weird Poets Society
Spillwords.com
Star*Line: The Journal Of The Science Fiction Poetry Association
Terror House Magazine
The Creeps Magazine
The Horror Zine
The Last Time: An Anthology
The Walking Dead: The Official Magazine
The Walking Dead Fans Facebook Group Page
2:00 A.M.: Poetry Facebook Group Page
Viral Disease Magazine
WordFest Anthology: Waco Cultural Arts Fest
Writing Texas Anthology
and
ZombiePoetryProject.com

Thank You to the Wonderfully Horrific Editors
who chose my zombie zonnets over others.

Zombie For Life!!!
(or death in this case)

Isaiah 9:20 NIV

*On the right they will devour, but still be hungry;
on the left they will eat, but not be satisfied.
Each will feed on the flesh of their own offspring.*

…with apologies to Stealers Wheels and their song,
"Stuck In The Middle With You"

*"Walkers to the left of me
Biters to the right
Here I am, running from zombies with you…"*

Table of Contents

Season One: Attack of The Zombie Zonnets 11
- Souls 13
- Wise 14
- Lights 15
- Translation 16
- Riverdale 17
- Supplies 18
- Letter 19
- Beginning 20
- Acts 21
- Lucille 22
- Music 23
- Perfect 24
- Rocket 25
- Remember 26
- Brains 27
- Inside 28
- Suddenly 29
- Explanation 30
- Herd 31
- Unmasked 32
- Shakes-fear 33
- Desire 34
- Truth 35
- Slave 36
- Walt-Mart 37

Season Two: Escape of the Zombie Zonnets 39
- Names 41
- Spanish 42
- Negan 43
- Rights 44

Altar	45
Flame	46
Ginger	47
Horseman	48
Knowledge	49
Plague	50
Road	51
Smiles	52
Twenty	53
Virus	54
UhhHHhh-UrrrrrR-MMmrR-RrAA -rRAAa-RaAAA!!:	55
Why Zombies Don't Like South Texas	56
War	57
Xenophobe	58
Yoga	59
Unexpected	60
Math	61
Kizz	62
Meat	63
Stereotypical	64
Life	65
Worry	66
Acknowledgements	67
About The Poet	71
(G)Rave Reviews	72

Season One

Attack of The Zombie Zonnets

Souls

Zombies don't have souls
That is why they walk like they do
If they didn't, then they wouldn't
So they walk in the only way that they walk

Zombies don't have souls
That is why they look like they do
If they didn't, then they wouldn't
So they look in the only way that they look

Zombies don't have souls
That is why they eat like they do
If they didn't, then they wouldn't
So they eat in the only way that they eat

Zombies don't have souls
How much more can you explain it?

Wise

A wise man once said:
An apple a day keeps the doctor away
A friend in need is a friend indeed
Attack is the best form of defense
An army marches on its stomach
Ask no questions and hear no lies

A wise man once said:
Actions speak louder than words
Adversity makes strange bedfellows
All things come to those who wait
All is well that ends well
As you sow, so shall you reap

A wise man once said all of these great things
Then something less wise ate him

Lights

Lights… yellow light, yellow light, yellow light…

Those traffic lights. Remember their purpose?
To control masses of humans in cars
Those miracles of steel and fiberglass
That now sit quietly in odd stages
In some sort of exodus from itself
Those were great times in human history

Now and then breaking the barren landscape
A vehicular carcass far from sway
Calling them to control with their straight lanes
In conventional progress to all sides
Now silent, gathering glances at best
From the mindless dead who pay them no mind

Red light, red light, red light, green light, green light…

Translation

Ooo grR ara rAaa ORrr ggGRRRR Rrrrrr araa!!
    I was a poet once beloved by some

arraaaa Ooo RoO Aahh ara RaA oRR gGgggRR OrR!!
    That I can hold no pen now matters not

GRR Ooo GrRRR orR ara MrRrr uUuuRr Rrrrrr RRaa!!
    For I crave not the sweet verses of life

sRrr ara RRaa UuUrrR Rrrrrr orRr RAaA UrrrRrRr!!
    But the sour juices of your deep thoughts

MMrrr GGrRRr araa rrRRAAA Rrrrrr ORrR Rraa!!
    Caged within the cranium of your soul

rrAA nuurg Ooooo ahHh sRRr Ooo rOoo aHH Orr MRrR!!
    Come to me dear and I will set you free

Ooo grR ara rAaa ORrr ggGRRRR Rrrrrr araa!!
    I was a poet once beloved by some

Riverdale

for the comic book series: Afterlife With Archie

Oh, Riverdale, sweet bygone Riverdale

Just to show you that it can happen here
To all the good people in this city
Like Archie, Betty, and Veronica
Even Jughead's canine is not immune
Cases of walking death in great places
Staining what was once wholesome, green, and good

What "it" was, they can't define for certain
Those outside the zombie box (for now) can
Person by person, house by house by house,
City by city, (panel by panel)
What tragic poems they will write about you
If there's anyone alive to write them

Oh, Riverdale, sweet bygone Riverdale

Supplies

Remember, just two weeks ago today
About all that muddle for some supplies
Ones you ordered early Monday morning
Ones you were supposed to receive Tuesday
They didn't come, but you waited a day
They still didn't come, so you called to ask
Ordered them again then waited once more
Thursday. They never came. Friday. The same
You called again, got usual runaround
They said you would have them by next Monday
Remember how angry you were those days
You tried to contain yourself, but you failed

How distant that seems now as you wrestle
Those same supplies from a postal zombie

Letter

To The Editor Of The Walking Dead Comic Book

It appears, according to your comic
book, that nobody famous survived the
zombie apocalypse! Why is that so?
I understand about intellectual
property and all that, but by now I
am sure you can afford it. Maybe keep
them alive for a few issues and then
kill him or her off. Or maybe even
a zombie that is recognizably
famous. Someone that you would be very
sympathetic to keeping around for
a while. You know, chained up somewhere just for
show. Kind of like some freaky-art display.
Yeah, I know, some weird, sick thoughts… But why not?

Beginning

Where were you when it all went down?
When we first fought for oil?
When the great towers fell?
When we went back to war?
When we first found out what really happened
Thirty years ago during Desert Storm?

Where were you when it all went down?
When it was first blamed on paganism?
When it was first blamed on bath salts?
When it was first blamed on synthetic marijuana?
When it was first blamed on man's devolution?
When CDC gave its first, real warning?

Where were you when it all went down?
When the zombies took out Cynthiana?

Acts

The act of walking
Makes one a walker
No matter how one does it or not
So one walks and walks and walks

The act of grabbing
Makes one a grabber
No matter how well one can hold on or not
So one grabs and grabs and grabs

The act of biting
Makes one a biter
No matter how good one is at it or not
So one bites and bites and bites

Well now, the act of all three makes one a zombie
So the rest of us just run and run and run

Lucille

What drives men to the point of their own end
Giving proper Christian names to objects
Lifeless, unable to care for themselves
Intimate with one's pain or one's pleasure
Baptizing them in precious, living blood
Or the walking carcass of what once was

What drives men to name inanimate things
That can't reason about their life or death
Nor distinguish between master or slave
Or nakedness, or arrogance, or sin
Or love, or hate, or fear, or conclusion
For sure, man has made this practice perfect

This machete. There are many like it.
But this one is mine. His name is Desi.

Music

They say the sound of silence
Is still itself a form of music
One that would be subtle and soft
Just below the pitch of your own breathing
We live in a world where silence is gone
Where it is a rare find of music indeed

With the sound of cell phones ringing and dinging
The hustle and bustle of human interaction
With the crowing and crooning of musicians
With the chitter chatter of the work place
With the whining of sirens and booming of planes
With loud, boisterous traffic; now all of it gone

Now listen to the gorging and gurgling of zombies
What is that music like? Heavy, death metal?

Perfect

In any world, zombies are perfection
They don't attack each other just because
They don't seem to mind sharing all their food
They don't cheat each other in anything
They don't fornicate and cause divisions
They don't discriminate one single bit

In any world, zombies are perfection
They don't try to hide what they really are
They don't even lie to anyone's face
They don't worry about what they look like
They don't hurry to where they are going
They don't waste time "getting to know you" well

Yes, in any world, zombies are perfect
Much better than most live humans I know

Rocket

The rich had hatched a plan to escape it
Priceless, a view onboard a rocket ship
Conception was mighty, the perfect plot
Ability and the means, all a plus
Food for decades for a human dozen
Life of the daring and now very scarce

Yet, how did they think they could avoid it
Dismissing facts regarding genetics
How it didn't matter how far you went
The turning disease rode within you
Like on earth, so in the vastness of space
Death but a doorway to a soulless drift

Into the dark vacuum of the cosmos
Flying squarely far to nowhere at all

Remember

Remember when
Your very skin craved for life
You longed to feel it in your hands
You thrived to touch it with your fingers
You wanted to embrace it forever
You had it all figured out

Remember when
Your life was simple, uncomplicated
You and your partner made lots of love
You had only normal life to worry about
You felt that you could live forever
You had it all figured out

Remember? Remember? Remember?
Dismember! Dismember! Dismember!

Brains

Zombies don't have brains
Because then it would remember
Tearing out the chest of its child
Tearing out the heart of its husband
Tearing out the mammary glands of its mother
Tearing out the face of its father
Tearing out the neck of its nephew

Zombies don't have brains
Because then it would remember
Tearing out the knuckles of its niece
Tearing out the ankles of its uncle
Tearing out the arms of its aunt
Tearing out the gallbladder of its grandfather
A baseball bat named "Lucille"

Inside

Inside of all of us
Every single one of us
Our human character
Our feelings, our emotions
Our essence, our spirit
All that makes us alive

Inside of all of us
Every single cell of life
Our love and losses
Our doing right, our doing wrong
Our strength, our weaknesses
All that makes us unique

Inside of all of us
Is a zombie waiting to come out

Suddenly

All of a sudden, you are interested
In the girl you used to call ugly
In the nerd you never wanted to talk too
In the postman making his delivery route
In the preacher condemning your very soul
In the groundskeeper cutting some brittle roses

All of a sudden, you are interested
In the farmer slowly milking the cows
In the sweaty guy pushing the lawnmower
In the policeman pointing a gun at you
In the way your mother is screaming away
In the odd poet and his so-called poetry

All of a sudden, you are so interested
In the way flesh will taste in your mouth

Explanation

Let me explain about those who eat brains
They must be mad or severely insane
They're clearly dead, nothing left in the head
No longer human, truly can be said

Let me explain about those who eat brains
They drag about slowly, never in pain
They move about quirky that is for sure
Whatever they have, for that there's no cure

Let me explain about those who eat brains
They'll eat a lot more and without complaint
Be dirty or clean, they won't care at all
Flesh is good eating, to them it's a ball

Let me explain about those who eat brains
Butt-naked or dressed, they just have no shame

Herd

Herd mentality, a precocious set
When those in masses have no mind at all
Irony, deep remnants of the senses
For years to no end after one has turned
Savoring what life has yet left to give
Despite stimulus of the spur of self

Do the cows feel the same for the green grass
Full of great, digestible minerals
As the dead do about the living flesh
Or is it more like the pack of grey wolves
Where they need to kill to eat and survive
No matter where it is or who it was

The stench of fresh, uncleansed, unsettled flesh
Drives the herd to quench their hunger madness

Unmasked

are you smarter than a zombie, I ask
because they most surely will outsmart you
their drive for flesh will push them beyond the task
they'll wait for days to see what you will do

are you smarter than a zombie, I ask
tunnel vision is the mechanism
controlling their lust, filling up their flask
preparing you for their next baptism

are you smarter than a zombie, I ask
for they were once, maybe smarter than you
not that there's anything under the mask
eternally affixed, doomed to the cue

are you smarter than a zombie, I ask
eternity waits for you to unmask

Shakes-fear

Zombie or not zombie is the query
That distracts the living in troubled times
For the dead have no thoughts nor any cares
Except for the insatiable hunger
That propels them without a single thought
Dreams stay dreams, only nightmares are fulfilled
The oppressed and the proud, all taste the same
Death now only matters to the fearful
Death is the grand prize you win to begin
The dead but walking carry no worries
Writers of history, stories, and poems
Among those that now search for human flesh
All of it to say that what matters now
Matters not at all but to few alive

Desire

I want to change my name to Almost-Joe-R.-Lansdale and speak truth about Texas and how to deal with the zombie virus.

I want to change my name to Not-Stephen-King-But-Close and just sit at home and write poems about zombies till my heart's content.

I want to change my name to Maybe-Dean-Koontz-Or-Maybe-Not and then tell stories about Frankenstein's monster's zombie past.

I want to change my name to Fake-H.-P.-Lovecraft and fill the oceans with new fear: zombies don't swim but they will float to you.

I want to change my name to earn a life talking about zombies and more zombies.

Truth

"I'm telling you the truth for the last time.
There is no such thing as a damned zombie.
That is just crap made up by Hollywood
to make money while scaring you to hell."

These were the very words I remember.
Now, with a muzzle covering your mouth
to keep you from snapping at me again,
I want to argue the point I made then.

Why don't you grunt to admit I was right?
The fact that you want to eat me proves it.
Now, I have to keep you chained up and safe.
Otherwise the living will destroy you.

Damn it, Bob! How'd you break that chain again?
Bob, listen man! I was just kidding!... Bob!

Slave

The questions on how it all happened
Don't matter much the way you see it
But it did happen and there is the truth
Although the truth today is far from setting you free

Before it all went down, you were going down
On any high-paying, Tom, Dick, and Hairless guy
You were enjoying the life, the pay, the attention
Before you realized you were tricked into the trade

Your benefactors, so long since gone
Like fresh customers and your humanity
Yet you still remain faithful to your old job
A slave as you grind whether dead or alive

But what does one pay the dead like you
Who gives out for free the final fellatio?

Walt-Mart

You used to love shopping there in the past
Now you despise it beyond what you know

You enjoyed the sweet smell from the bake shop
The free reading from the magazine rack
The tasting of fresh fruits that weren't samples
The trying of clothes that you weren't buying

You enjoyed the scenery just as well
Critiquing skinny jeans as you strolled by
Those good-looking girls in their spandex pants
In their waist-high skirts or their skimpy shorts

Yes, you always liked going there to shop
Certainly now, you'd rather go elsewhere
Battling the undead through the long aisles
To get to the canned corn is far too much

Season Two

Escape of the Zombie Zonnets

Names

Whether you call them
meat puppets, or walkers,
or them, or lurkers,
or empties, or floaters,
or lame-brains, or roamers,
or herd of biters,
or monsters, or snappers,
or pets, or creepers,
or soulless, or shufflers,
or zombies, or chewers,
or undead, or restless,
or plane ol' walking dead

Whatever you want to call them now
They used to have real and formal names

Spanish

"*¡Los muertos viven!*" in broken Spanish
Finally taking the effort to learn it
A language you never wanted to speak
Your "agenda" placed you way above it
Remember you said it was beneath you
Look at you now in this disturbing age

Problem though; it don't matter anymore
Fear sounds the same in any damned language
The undead don't care how you speak to them
Or how sweet this speech now appears to you
You know it's all about "brain-love" with "them"
Plus, Spanish-speaking locals are smiling

It only takes one to distract the hordes
Guess who they're saying they're knocking down first?

Negan

when Negan escapes from jail in The Walking Dead #153

Where o' where is this evil-heart, Negan?
Where o' where could he ever gone too?
Follow the corpses that lay at your feet
Follow the path that is clearest to you

Where o' where is this nasty-mind, Negan?
Where o' where? Will your chances be slim?
Follow the puddle and rivers of blood
Follow the evil that leads you to him

Where o' where is this stealthy-swift, Negan?
Where o' where will there be such an end?
Follow your heart as he tears it apart
Follow your mind as he bashes it in

If you can't find him, don't beat yourself blue
For somewhere Negan is looking for you

Rights

walking from my grave just to place my vote
humans avoid me like an ancient plague
giving me all the space of a large boat
it intoxicates as my mind grows vague

will have to ask somebody for a hand
because both of mine fell off on the way
maintain your distance my delicious man
this little cough will mess up a good day

putting all politicians on notice
i've still got rights, i still got my duty
more than enough reasons to scare "potus"
dead or alive, this vote is a beauty

i'll make it count good, nail that coffin shut
then I'll start feasting on everyone's guts

Altar

here at the Altar of the Tub
where we shed our own blood
so that humanity can live on
here at Terminus, O' Terminus

here at the Altar of the Tub
behind the sacred fences
where humanity holds on tight
here at Terminus, O' Terminus

here at the Altar of the Tub
why sacrifice for the dead out there
when you can do it for us in here
at Terminus, O' Terminus

kneel at the Altar of the Tub
where your blood will flow in the flood

Flame

I remember when we were in high school
reeling in the heat of the first flame
the youth, the exhaustion, the passion
the intense yearning and raw tenderness
like innocent rabbits without regard
having our intimate way with ourselves

presently, beyond those amazing years
within the largest closet in the house
wearing the same chains our dog once wore
lunging at me every time she sees me
offering the freshest of meat to be found
as it becomes rarer each time I hunt

death seems forever, but I kept my part
sex, however, is now a bit awkward

Ginger

the last time… the last time I saw Ginger
was on a stripper pole at The Palace
a skin joint halfway down Everhart Lane
where I used to go when things were normal

the last time… the last time I talked to her
she seemed interested in my attention
if the price was right, the party was on
open to any direction I chose

the last time… the last time she left the floor
she'd agreed to all my verbal requests
with a sweet wink, she blew a kiss my way
as she darted into the powder room

the last time… the last time I saw her next
she's walking my way no longer alive

Horseman

half of him is still mounted on a horse
not much left of the mount, for that matter
somehow, it still works for the both of them
a third of the man's head clearly missing
a snarling carnation of Jonah Hex
he holds the reigns of two-thirds of the steed
still with most of its once, powerful legs
muscle rippling through roughly torn skin
there's nothing religious about all this
they're not collecting souls, they're just hungry
like some headless horseman nightmare of old
they're waiting on you, they want you to run
just to feed on exhausted, sweaty flesh
even if your skin's tougher than leather

Knowledge

what if it was all backwardly written
what is lost at times in the translation
from one sharp language with very strong rules
to another with its own verbiage strength
yet still others in line between the two
with dialects playing in the matter

what if what is written in holy texts
has been accidently changed through the times
where those with the engraved mark of the beast
as described in the end chapter of life
were the ones not allowed to shop in stores
conduct business as normal, live in peace

what if the proverbial marker is just
simple temperature readings of illness

Plague

the truth is hard, you just can't escape it
hell, it is on every TV station
every Facebook post, every Instagram

can't seem to find an answer anywhere
our world is falling apart, piece by piece
race to the end, trying to slow it down
only to find a second wave coming
never will man understand the cycle
always balancing the order of things

very likely to wipe half of us out
indicating horrific projections
returning to levels of yesteryear
unless we stop all we are doing now
solutions that will keep with nature's rules

Road

"Why did the zombie cross the road?" you ask
well it wasn't a chicken, so there's that
but you are standing vibrantly alive
with a delicious heart and supple lungs
with salty moisture on your healthy skin
with well-kept thighs that make him cry mercy
looking quite helpless just across the road

"Why did the zombie cross the road?" you ask
what? are you stupid? you know what he wants
standing so provocatively human
his mouth waters in anticipation
as he dead-dreams about sinking his teeth
into your adrenalized, fear-filled flesh
yeah, you know you are just asking for it

Smiles

I used to love her deep, dark, gothic look
her down-with-America temperament
the conspiracist I fell in love with
but lately she has been smiling a lot

I remember just a few weeks ago
she was grumpy, bitchy, just complaining
about this or that, her lively parents
her exes, the taxes, the president

while I agreed with her on some of these
I drew the line when it came to my work
that my words were better left unwritten
and she has been smiling ever since then

well, it is more like a flesh-eating grin
but she seems happy chained to the garage

Twenty

Welcome Back to the Hundred Acre Wood
except now it's beat-down to the last ten
where Pooh Bear has hard-core diabetes
continuing dialysis, about to
loose his other leg, where gray Eeyore
has been cutting himself, even tried to
hang by the neck more than five times last year
where Tigger the Tiger's abuse of high
energy drinks has run its course as he
endures severe mange, even erectile
dysfunction, where sweet Piglet was just sold
to an exotic market harvesting
bacon, where fucking zombies still roam free
Yeah, it ain't that great anymore, Chris

Virus

the virus is in all of us
every arm pit, every ankle
every mouth, every nose
every arm, every leg
every ear, every eye
every breast, every thigh

the virus is in all of us
every foot, every hand
every brain, every belly
every man, every woman
every front, every fanny
every crook, every cranny

the virus is in all of us
waiting to be born from DEATH

UhhHHhh-UrrrrrR-MMmrR-RrAA -rRAAa-RaAAA!!:

mRR!!
mRR!!
mRR!!
...rAaaAA gGgGRrR!!

mRR!!
mRR!!
mRR!!
...rAaaAA gGgGRrR!!

mRR!!
mRR!!
mRR!!
...rAaaAA gGgGRrR!!

mRR!!
...rAaaAA gGgGRrR!!

Why Zombies Don't Like South Texas

[*Translation of "UhhHHhh-UrrrrrR-MMmrR-RrAA -rRAAa-RaAAA!!:"*]

hot
hot
hot
...turkey buzzards

hot
hot
hot
...turkey buzzards

hot
hot
hot
...turkey buzzards

hot
...turkey buzzards

War

formerly called the hidden enemy
yet in plain sight, waited to attack man

where he could barely measure its distance
he could surely place value on effect
a number beyond astronomical
a cost never seen before on this earth
some would blame it on the wrath of a god
but it surely was not scripted that way
in any holy book found on this world
or in the artifacts found on the moon
this was not the work of man-creator
this was the creation of man himself

nothing hidden about it in these days
as it freely stutter-marches outside

Xenophobe

what are you afraid of, fellow human
were you not looking to the stars for life
searching for the answers to loneliness

were you not trying to communicate
with dolphins to find intrepid mermaids
well up until they stopped talking to man

were you not engaging in all matters
of finding that which looked and talked like you
or something quite close to that idea

yet when it fell into your blue oceans
in flames from a far-away, unknown place
reconstituting to its former self

you were repugnant at the thought of it
up until it took your form and ate you

Yoga

the fitness center remains wide open
in the middle of this huge messed-up world
giving the allegorical finger
to a swift, life-altering contagion

running on long-lasting generators
new ones powered by solar energy
the video screens on a constant loop
allowed for all genres of fitness flicks

they like the ones with techno pop music
they go ape-shit for the faster rock tunes
the Fonda tapes confuse them to no end
but the yoga ones seem to calm them down

keep in mind walking through the sea of death
the five-minute breaks could get real hairy

Unexpected

In the middle of a Black Friday Sale
It happened: Biblical Resurrection
Leaving behind cold, empty, human shells
Without souls, without trace of human life
Indentured as locusts thus prophesied
Their stinging bite will endure eternal
Repentance is acceptance, but it's late
Revelations moves forward at their pace
You will run far, still they will sniff you out
They will tear your flesh, yet you will not die
Prayer might help if vocal cords remain
Life has been your own making to this point
Your Creator has let you do your will
Now you wonder if it was worth it all

Math

in summation of pandemic outbreak
where a dark government sponsored agent
has altered our biological state
the need for additional provisions
is now a question about life or death

you and a small party head to Zone B
to appropriate medical supplies
to deliver to Zone D in three days
along the way to the very next point
you lose three in a five-biter attack
leaving Zone A you lose another three
as you are surprised by fifteen roamers

you and one other safely reach Zone D
she just bit you… man, this word problem sucks

Kizz

a zombified KISS song

Tonight, I wanna' eat all of you
With this sickness, there's so much that I will do
And tonight, I wanna' eat even your feet
'Cause, baby, I was meant for this
And, baby, you taste good to me

I was meant for eating you, baby
You were meant as food for me
And I can't eat enough of you, baby
Can you stop so I can eat?

Tonight, I wanna' see terror in those eyes
Feel the tragedy, the fear that makes me smile
And tonight, I'm gonna' make your worries all come true
'Cause, baby, I was meant for this
And, baby, you taste good to me

Meat

Remember your job, how your boss treats you
your co-workers and their constant issues
about how you can't keep up with demands
in the end, you are just a piece of meat

Remember your wife, how your kids behave
even your dog has lost respect for you
and your cat, well they have expectations
in the end, you are just a piece of meat

Remember your dreams, how they were shattered
everyone constantly telling you that
dreams are worthless, but hey, so are you
in the end, you are just a piece of meat

Remember in the end when the dead rise
clearly. you'll still BE just a piece of meat

Stereotypical

Trying not to be, but I can't help it
You can pretty much tell who is or not
I mean, who moans about work constantly?
Who is always trying to get so close?
Who is always struggling to walk or talk?
Who is always late to our group meetings?

I tell you, I know one when I see one
So if I see something, I'll do something
That something on this list: Ricardo
He is a zombie if ever there was
I mean, look at him. He dresses funny.
He smells horrible. He says my name weird.

I just know I'm right! So who is with me?
Let's vote to see who will bash his brains in

Life

Another day above ground, they would say
Was another great day of life, of health

What satire these days for those still alive
What pleasures in life can be found today
What is worth at all in this existence
What purpose does life even matter now
Where children are the rarest find indeed
Where there is no long-distanced time to love
For relationships, for settling down
For there is only time to survive here
For they will come one day. They will find you
For they will wait until your last mistake

Gone, as we know it. These last days of us.
These last days of man. These last days of life.

Worry

We used to worry that the sky would fall
About the big hole in the atmosphere
About the nukes that would come to kill us
Even how much we would pay for cable

We used to worry about the cancers
About the innumerable diseases
About the rich, the poor, the racism
Even what made us look skinny or fat

We used to worry about worrying
About the effect it had on humans…
Then everything went eerily quiet
Then we became the united species

Now we share one universal worry
To walk as the living or the undead

Acknowledgements

Acts (Episode 1.9) first appeared in *The Walking Dead: The Official Magazine #15 (2016).*

Altar (Episode 2.5) first appeared in *The Walking Dead Fans Facebook Group Page (2020)* as "Altar Of The Tub."

Beginning (Episode 1.8) first appeared in *ZombiePoetryProject.com (2016).*

Brains (Episode 1.15) first appeared in *Rat's Ass Review (2019).*

Desire (Episode 1.22) first appeared in *Star*Line: The Journal Of The Science Fiction Poetry Association, Issue 43.1 (2020).*

Explanation (Episode 1.18) first appeared in *Terror House Magazine (2019).*

Flame (Episode 2.6) first appeared in the *WordFest Anthology 2020: Waco Cultural Arts Fest (2020).*

Ginger (Episode 2.7) first appeared in *Blood Moon Rising Magazine #81 (2020).*

Herd (Episode 1.19) first appeared in *The Horror Zine (2020)* as "Herd: A Zombie Zonnet."

Horsman (Episode 2.8) first appeared in *Blood Moon Rising Magazine #81 (2020).*

Inside (Episode 1.16) first appeared in *Spillwords.com (2019).*

Kizz (Episode 2.21) first appeared in *Viral Disease Magazine 2020)* as "I Was Meant For Eating You!"

Knowledge (Episode 2.9) first appeared in the *Fallen Angel Poetry Facebook Group Page* (2020).

Letter (Episode 1.7) first appeared in the *Red River Review (2017)* as "Letter To The Editor Of The Walking Dead Comic Book As A Prose Sonnet."

Life (Episode 2.24) first appeared in the *Poetry Universe Facebook Group Page (2020)* as "Life: A Zombie Zonnet."

Lights (Episode 1.3) first appeared in a *Horror Writers Association Online Interview (2017)*.

Lucille (Episode 1.10) first appeared in *Bleached Butterfly (2019)*.

Math (Episode 2.20) first appeared in *Boundless: The Anthology Of The Rio Grande Valley International Poetry Festival (2020)*.

Meat (Episode 2.22) first appeared in *Speculations II: Poetry From The Weird Poets Society 2019 (2020)*.

Music (Episode 1.11) first appeared in *Bleached Butterfly (2019)*.

Names (Episode 2.1) first appeared in *Harbinger Asylum (2020)* as "Names: A Zombie Zonnet."

Negan (Episode 2.3) first appeared in *Blood Moon Rising Magazine #78 (2020)* as "Finding Negan."

Perfect (Episode 1.12) first appeared in *The Horror Zine (2019)*.

Plague (Episode 2.10) first appeared in the *At Home Anthology (2020)*.

Remember (Episode 1.14) first appeared in the *Horror Zine (2019)*.

Rights (Episode 2.4) first appeared in the *Poetry Society Of Texas Facebook Group Page (2020)* as "Zombie Voting Rights: A Zombie Zonnet."

Riverdale (Episode 1.5) first appeared in *The Horror Zine (2019)*.

Road (Episode 2.11) first appeared in *Spillwords.com (2020)*.

Rocket (Episode 1.13) first appeared in *The Creeps Magazine #21 (2019) as* "Rocket To Nowhere."

Shakes-Fear (Episode 1.21) first appeared in *The Horror Zine (2020) as* "Shakes-Fear: A Zombie Zonnet."

Slave (Episode 1.24) first appeared in *Terror House Magazine (2020)*.

Smiles (Episode 2.12*)* first appeared in *Terror House Magazine (2020)*.

Souls (Episode 1.1) first appeared in *Writing Texas (2016-2017)*.

Spanish (Episode 2.2) first appeared in *Blood Moon Rising Magazine #78 (2020)*.

Stereotypical (Episode 2.23) first appeared in *Screw The Wall! And Other Brown People Poems* (2020) as "Stereotypical: A Zombie Poem… Or Is It?"

Suddenly (Episode 1.17) first appeared in *Spillwords.com (2019)*.

Supplies (Episode 1.6) first appeared in *The Horror Zine (2019)*.

Translation (Episode 1.4) first appeared in a *Horror Writers Association Online Interview (2017)*.

Truth (Episode 1.23) first appeared in *The Last Time: An Anthology (2020)*.

Twenty (Episode 2.13) first appeared in *Terror House Magazine (2020)* as "Twenty Years Much Later."

UhhHHhh-UrrrrrR-MMmrR-RrAA -rRAAa-RaAAA!!: (Episode 2.14) first appeared in the 2:00 A.M.: Poetry Facebook Group Page (2020) as "UhhHHhh-UrrrrrR-MMmrR-RrAA –rRAAa-RaAAA!!:/Why Zombies Don't Like South Texas."

Unexpected (Episode 2.19) first appeared in *Corpus Christi Writers Anthology (2020)*.

Unmasked (Episode 1.20) first appeared in *The Horror Zine* as "Unmasked: A Zombie Zonnet" (2020).

Virus (Episode 2.15) first appeared in *Blood Moon Rising Magazine #81 (2020)*.

Walt-Mart (Episode 1.25) first appeared in *Terror House Magazine (2020)*.

War (Episode 2.16) first appeared in *Terror House Magazine (2020)*.

Wise (Episode 1.2) first appeared in *Writing Texas (2016-2017)*.

Worry (Episode 2.25) first appeared in *Rattle's Anything Goes Poetry Facebook Page (2020)* as "Worry: A Zombie Zonnet."

Xenophobe (Episode 2.17) first appeared in *Red Planet Magazine #9 (2020)*.

Yoga (Episode 2.18) first appeared in the *Poetry Super Highway Facebook Group Page (2020)*.

About The Poet

Juan Manuel Pérez, a Mexican-American poet of indigenous descent and the current Poet Laureate for Corpus Christi, Texas (2019-2020), is the author of Another Menudo Sunday (2007), O' Dark Heaven: A Response to Suzette Haden Elgin's Definition of Horror (2009), WUI: Written Under the Influence of Trinidad Sanchez, Jr. (2011), Live From La Pryor: The Poetry of Juan Manuel Perez: A Zavala Country Native Son, Volume 1 (2014), Sex, Lies, and Chupacabras (2015), Space In Pieces (2020), and Screw The Wall! And Other Brown People Poems (2020), as well as, the co-editor of The Call Of The Chupacabra (2018). He is the 2011-2012 San Antonio Poets Association Poet Laureate and the Lone Star State's only EL Chupacabras Poet Laureate (For Life). The former Gourd Dancer for the Memphis Tia Piah Big River Clan Warrior Society is also a Pushcart Prize Nominee as well as a SEATTAH Scholar (Striving For Excellence And Accountability In The Teaching Of Traditional American History) through the University Of Dallas. Juan is a ten-year Navy Corpsman/Combat Marine Medic with experience in the 1991 Persian Gulf War (Operations Desert Shield, Desert Storm, and Desert Calm) with the 2nd Marines and the 1992 Hurricane Andrew Relief Marine Air Group Task Force. This two-time Teacher of the Year, along with his wife, Malia (a three-time Teacher of the Year), is a co-founder of The House of the Fighting Chupacabras Press. The former migrant field worker previously from La Pryor, currently worships his Creator, teaches public high school history, writes poetry, and chases chupacabras in the Texas Coastal Bend Area.

His official website is **https://juanmperez.weebly.com/**

(G)Rave Reviews

Juan Perez pulls off the impressive feat of revisiting the popular zombie trope and putting a new spin on it, creating a world where the zombies are here to save us from ourselves. Writing with poignancy, power, and wit, Perez's zombie poems highlight the humanity that drops away when we give in to our contemporary knee-jerk compulsion toward Othering. The voice of Perez's zombies, like that of their creator, demands an audience, grabs you by the throat and whispers "see me; love me" before taking a bite.

—Paul Juhasz, author of Fulfillment: Diary of a Warehouse Picker… and a Zombie Fan

Perez is able to capture the perspective of life as a zombie, developing the concept that reality is not much different than the horrific and gory tales of Zombie culture and Pop Culture crossovers in between. As Perez puts it, "Let me explain about those who eat brains, Butt-naked or dressed, they have no shame". Incredibly descriptive to create visuals to compare reality to Perez's Zombtopia. This collection of his Zombie Zonnets is a must read for those interested in anything Zombies (or even the slightest bit curious).

—Marah Perez, Poet, Cosplayer, Science Teacher, and Zombie-ologist

Juan Perez has taken zombies where they've never been before…into a zonnet; and I like it. Zombie Zonnets Season One introduces us to zombies we know and love (think The Walking Dead) and zombies we learn to love. Whether they are in the "Acts" of walking, grabbing, or biting, or making "Music", they are almost likeable. Of course, the human response to "Rocket" ourselves away or just run and run is addressed. No matter, we keep coming back to the zonnets for more. As an avid fan of the television show, and a latecomer to the graphic novels, I love how Perez has interwoven moments from both into these zonnets. "Inside" parallels the moment at the lab when the scientist tells Rick the virus is in all of us. Our favorite non-human character, Lucille, makes an appearance in "Brains" and the eponymous "Lucille." We run into some non-dead characters as well. This collection is a great addition to the collection of any zombie or The Walking Dead fan. You will laugh at some of these zonnets, nod along in agreement with others. Mostly, you will be glad you're not part of the zombie horde, for "The stench of fresh, uncleansed, unsettled flesh/Drives the herd to quench their hunger madness."

> —Karen Tardiff, Editor for Gnashing Teeth Publishing, Poet, and Fan of The Walking Dead

This poetry collection is deceptively entertaining. Whether intentional or not, each piece is a multilayered snapshot of a variety of experiences. The reader can take each poem at face value and find a humorous commentary or sarcastic wit, but can also dig deeper and find that nearly each poem in this short collection can reveal some honest commentary on the shared human experience. Thematically, zombies are often used as a way to reveal that the thing we as humans fear the most is ourselves. George Romero, the father of modern zombie films, famously explained that his Day of The Dead film was a way to highlight how modern human obsession with consumerism was as destructive to ourselves as any horror beast might be. In a similar fashion, Perez uses "Walmart" to show the level of access we have to just about anything is taken for granted and yet, the illusion of "consumer choice" is still present in the apocalypse! The delicate balance of thoughtful nuance and the appearance of intentional dry humor delivery is something to be appreciated. Several pieces in this collection are revealing in that they pose the questions of what it means to be a human in this modern world, and compare that definition to a zombie...only to find there are more similarities than differences. Pieces like "Herd" and "Unmasked" aren't afraid to be predictable, after all humans and zombies are predictable, again revealing similarities over differences. As complex as we believe ourselves to be, Perez finds ways to simplify this inner dialogue with pieces like "Perfect", "Desire", and "Music", almost as a critique telling us not to make it harder than it has to be. Where "Perfect" and "Desire" might serve as an allegory to not being ourselves and being better, "Music" and "Supplies" remind us to appreciate the things we have now, all with a dash of humor. Of course, you can't have someone write about zombies and not overtly lean into the genre. "Translation", "Brains", and "Explanation" are great examples of this. Overall, Perez surprises with the diversity of tones and imagery that this collection presents. It is certainly a work that one can devour and enjoy. After all, as Perez writes, we all have a little bit of zombie "Inside".

—Mike Quintanilla, Artist, Entrepreneur, and Zombie Aficionado